— What Shape Is a Poem? —

What Shape Is a Poem? is Paul's fifteenth anthology for Macmillan Children's Books.

When he's not editing fantastic collections like this Paul spends most of his time visiting schools, festivals and so on to perform his work and lead workshops. At present he visits well over a hundred schools every year.

Paul performs regularly with David Harmer in the poetry duo *Spill the Beans* and plays five a side football twice a week. Unlike this book he wishes he were in better shape.

If there's any time left he spends it with his wife Sally and two children – Sam and Daisy – in sunny Retford.

Other books from Macmillan

The Works
Every kind of poem you will ever need for
the Literacy Hour
Chosen by Paul Cookson

Don't Get Your Knickers in a Twist
Poems chosen by Paul Cookson

The Works 2
Poems for every subject and for every occasion
Chosen by Brian Moses and Pie Corbett

The School Year
Three terms of poems chosen by Brian Moses

The Very Best of Paul Cookson
Poems by Paul Cookson

The Evil Dr Mucus Spleen
and other superbad villains
Poems chosen by Paul Cookson

What Shape Is a Poem?

Poems chosen by
Paul Cookson

MACMILLAN CHILDREN'S BOOKS

*To all my friends at North Border Junior School – thanks.
Ten years of visits . . . and counting! You know
the poems better than me.*

First published 2002 by Macmillan Children's Books
a division of Macmillan Publishers Limited
20 New Wharf Road, London N1 9RR
Basingstoke and Oxford
www.panmacmillan.com

Associated companies throughout the world

ISBN 0 330 39707 9

3 5 7 9 8 6 4 2

A CIP catalogue record for this book is available from
the British Library.

Designed and illustrated by Jason Cox
Printed and bound in Great Britain by Mackays of Chatham plc, Kent

— Contents —

My Rocket Ship	*Ian Bland*	1
Buzz In	*Liz Brownlee*	2
Step by Step	*Paul Bright*	3
Electric Guitars	*James Carter*	4
It's Here It's There	*Paul Cookson*	5
Ball Bouncing	*John Foster*	6
Perform Somersaults	*Richard Caley*	8
It's Raining	*Paul Cookson*	10
Careful When You Pour	*Paul Cookson*	11
Black Hole	*Jane Clarke*	12
Pyramid	*Dave Calder*	13
In the Bath	*Andrew Collett*	14
CARtoon	*Gina Douthwaite*	15
Child Skipping	*John Foster*	16
Spaced Out	*Trevor Harvey*	17
BAKED BEANS:		
SPECIAL OFFER	*Mike Johnson*	18
Undersea Tea	*Tony Mitton*	19
Moon Journey	*Patricia Leighton*	20
Choir	*Ian McMillan*	21
Why are trees like the post office?	*Eric Petrie*	22
The Hiccup	*Coral Rumble*	23
With Reference to a Walk	*Coral Rumble*	24
After School	*Roger Stevens*	26
A Golfing Success	*Fred Sedgwick*	27
Vacuum Cleaner	*James Carter*	28

— Contents —

Dennis	*James Carter*	29
Belt	*John Foster*	30
The Open Gate	*Alan Watkins-Groves*	31
Diamond Poem	*John Foster*	32
Size Poem	*Roger Stevens*	33
The River	*James Carter*	34
Mexican Wave	*Philip Burton*	35
Sweet Dreams	*Ian Bland*	36
Calligrams	*Ian Bland*	37
Aaaah!!!! At Last it's Spring!!!!	*James Carter*	38
Well-known Proverb	*Paul Cookson*	39
Swallow	*Tony Charles*	40
Africa	*Dave Calder*	41
Shoe, Boot! Shoe!	*Gina Douthwaite*	42
Concrete Poems	*John Foster*	43
Helter-skelter	*Mike Johnson*	44
Run	*Roger Stevens*	45
The House Hunter	*Jill Townsend*	46
The Christmas Pudding	*Patricia Leighton*	47
Christmas Decoration	*James Carter*	48
Christmas Eve	*Liz Brownlee*	49
Well-known Song Title	*Paul Cookson*	50
Family Tree	*Damian Harvey*	51
Crossword Puzzle	*Paul Cookson*	52
The Shape of a Poem	*Chris Ogden*	54
There's No Other Letter	*Suzanne Elvidge*	56

— Contents —

o the wonderful shape of an o Rachel Rooney 57

Untidy Poem Roger Stevens 58

Seated David Petts 59

Watch this Space! Judith Nicholls 60

Tall Story Mike Johnson 61

Teeth Cleaning Poem Sue Cowling 62

Icicle Sue Cowling 63

Knickers Gina Douthwaite 64

How Playtime Shapes Up Chris Ogden 65

Toboggan David Whitehead 66

Owl Sandy Brownjohn 67

Lightning Strikes Damian Harvey 68

Begins with 'B' Gina Douthwaite 69

Building a Bonfire from the
    Bottom Up Angela Topping 70

Whalespout Sue Cowling 71

A Ride Debjani Chatterjee 72

Bonfire David Petts 73

Dream Ian McMillan 74

Purrfect Liz Brownlee 75

Acknowledgements 77

— My Rocket Ship —

Today I made
A rocket ship
That can fly
Me to the stars.
It's made from
Plastic bottles
Cardboard boxes
And jam jars.
Its engine is a
Broken Clock,
That was left under the stairs.
The seats are made from socks and shirts
That no one ever wears.

Ian Bland

Bee
arrives
bee jives
bee dives in
Bee hive

Liz Brownlee

— Step by Step —

Start at the bottom

I just wish the board weren't quite so high!

Try

And I'll

I'd do it

Said

Diving into the swimming pool

Cool

I'm so

Them

I'd show

Thought

Keep my big mouth shut?

Why don't I

Nut

Kind of

Some

Be

I must

Paul Bright

— Electric Guitars —

I like electric guitars:
played mellow or moody
frantic or fast – on CDs
or tapes, at home or in
cars – live in the streets,
at gigs or in bars.
I like
electric
guitars:
played
choppy
l i k e
reggae
or angry
l i k e
rock or
chirpy
l i k e
jazz or
strummy
l i k e
pop or
h e a v y
l i k e
metal – it
bothers
me not.

I like electric guitars:
their strings and their straps
and their wild wammy bars – their
jangling and twanging and funky
wah-wahs – their fuzz boxes,
frets and multi-effects –
pick-ups, machine
heads, mahogany necks
– their plectrums, their wires
and big amplifiers. I like electric
guitars: played loudly, politely – dully
or brightly – daily or nightly – badly
or nicely. I like electric guitars:
bass, lead and rhythm –
I basically dig 'em –

I like electric guitars

James Carter

4

It's here it's there
it's all around the room
I wish I'd knotted
my balloooo...

oooooo
ooooooo
oooooooo
ooooooooo
ooooooo
ooonnnnnnnnn

Paul Cookson

BALL BALL BALL BALL BALL BALL BALL BALL BALL BALL BA WALL

John Foster

To score a ten upon the

vault you must perform a somersault

Richard Caley

9

— It's Raining —

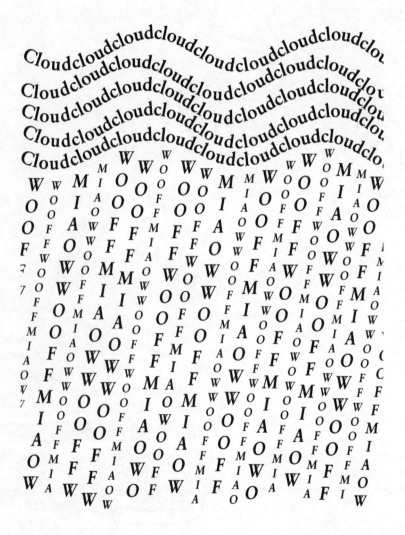

Paul Cookson

— Careful When You Pour —

Start at the bottom

PPPPPPPPPPPPPPPPPPPPPPPP
PPPPPPPPPPPPPPPPPPPP
PPPPPPPPPPPPPPPPPP
PPPPPPPPPPPPPPPP
PPPPPPPPPPPPPP
PPPPPPPPPP
PPPPPP

right over the toppppppp
bubble bubble froth trouble
bubble bubble froth trouble
bubble bubble froth trouble
is it time to stop...?
plink plink hisss hisss
right up to the top
pour me very gently
fizzy whizzy pop
liberate the carbonated
do not spill a drop
gurgle gurgle splish splash

Paul Cookson

11

— Black Hole —

Start here
read clockwise

What's the matter?
Vacuum cleaner!
A star is dying
releasing forces
terrifying
Old red giant
huge and shiny
collapses.
Now he's dense and tiny
Gravity
becoming meaner.
Universal

Jane Clarke

12

P
EAK
PLACE
PROUDLY
PROVIDING
PRESTIGIOUS
PLUSH PRIVATE
PILED PENTHOUSE
PERFECTLY PLANNED
PANORAMIC POSITION
PART PAYMENT POSSIBLE
PAST PHARAOHS PREFERRED

Dave Calder

— In the Bath —

When I pull
the plug out
with my round
and wrinkly toe,
the water likes
as it disappears
to gurgle
below

Andrew Collett

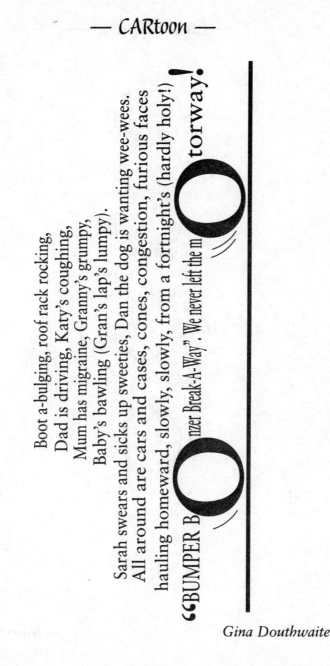

Boot a-bulging, roof rack rocking,
Dad is driving, Katy's coughing,
Mum has migraine, Granny's grumpy,
Baby's bawling (Gran's lap's lumpy).
Sarah swears and sicks up sweeties, Dan the dog is wanting wee-wees.
All around are cars and cases, cones, congestion, furious faces
hauling homeward, slowly, slowly, from a fortnight's (hardly holy!)
"BUMPER Bonzer Break-A-Way". We never left the motorway!

Gina Douthwaite

15

— Child Skipping —

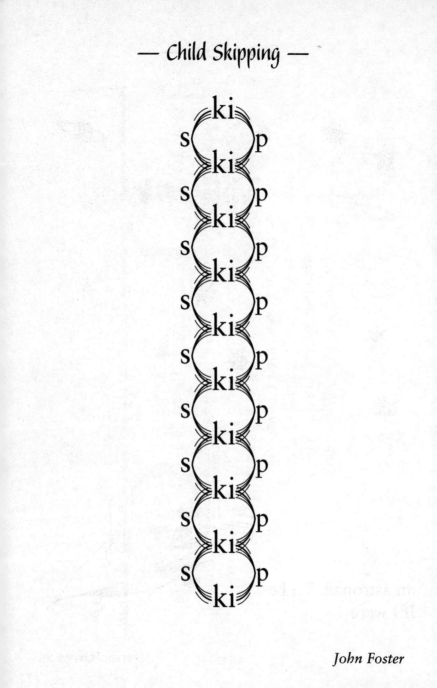

John Foster

Start at the bottom

Milky Way

with a taste for the

r
e
y
l
f

h
g
i
h

a

an astronaut I'd be
If I were

Trevor Harvey

Mike Johnson

— Undersea Tea —

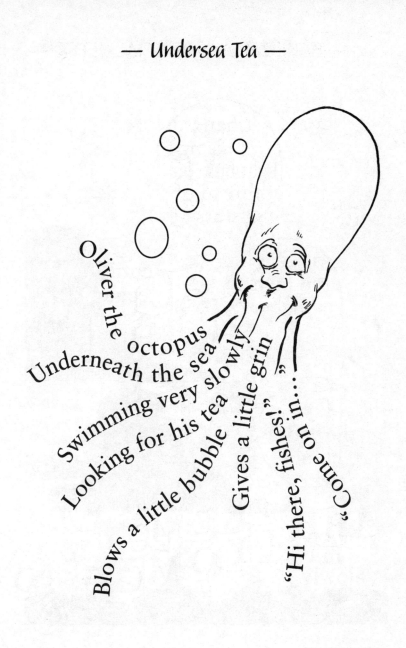

Oliver the octopus
Underneath the sea
Swimming very slowly
Looking for his tea
Blows a little bubble
Gives a little grin
"Hi there, fishes!"
"Come on in..."

Tony Mitton

— Moon Journey —

It hangs,
a pulsing
light bulb on a
thread of
stars

it goes.
and higher
Higher

until the
edge of
a cloud

sky.
the velvet
climbs

puts it out.

moon
a full
Slowly

Patricia Leighton

— Choir —

OOOOOOOOOOO
OOOOOOOOOOO
OOOOOOOOOOO
OOOOOOOOOOO

Choir in Winter

OOOOOCHOOOOOOO
OCHOOOCHOOOOOO
CHOOCHOOACHOOO
ACHOOCHOOACHOO

Choir with Sore Throats

oooooooooooooooooooooo
oooo ooooo oooooooooo
o o o o   oooooooooo
o o o o oooooo

Choir with Two New Members

OOOOOOOOOOOOOOO
OOOOOOOAOOOOOO
OOOOOOOOOOOEOO
OOOOOOOOOOOOOO

Choir Attacked by Wasps

OOOZZOOZOOZOOZOZO
ZZOOZOZOZOZOZZZZOO
ZZZZOOOOZZZOOZZOZO

Ian McMillan

— Why are trees like the post office? They've got branches everywhere —

I don't think
I could ever see   a poem written like a tree
words make up poems and branches make up trees
the leaves hang around looking bored
on those branches which make up the trees while poems hang around yawning
at the back of branches of w. h. smith's – forever unsold until in their autumn
the leaves – the   pages – turn brown at the edges   and curl; the glue dries
and the leaves fall out of the books and are swept away unread
and those bits of   poems – letters – I am the   alpha and the beta;
punctuation – breathy commas, detective constable question mark interrogating suspects? – dashes
racing off into the   distance – and exclamation marks make you shriek with excitement!
and words: words that sound cuddly, snuggle down with a nice megatherium;   words
that menace, seeyoustitchthatpal; words that love you, hold you safe and
chase off the monsters; words that are diamond – hard and shiny; words that are duvet – sleepy
and golden – words   emerging from some primal alphabet soup – are bits of poems swept up
into bin bags never to be seen again?   or in the spring   does new life
spring up,   spring to attention, spring out, spring to life?
for poems are green,   and make pictures
of the world
we live in
and make
some sense
of our rootless lives.

perhaps, a poem is written like a tree. growing forever. adding daily new leaves to the poet-tree.

Eric Petrie

— The Hiccup —

Hic ^{cup,} hic ^{cup,} hic ^{cup,}

Hic ^{cup,} hic ^{cup,} hic ^{cup,}

Hic ^{cup,} hic ^{cup,} hic ^{cup,}

Hic ^{cup,} hic ^{cup,} hic ^{cup,}

Hic ^{cup,} hic ^{cup,} hic ^{cup,}

Thanks

Coral Rumble

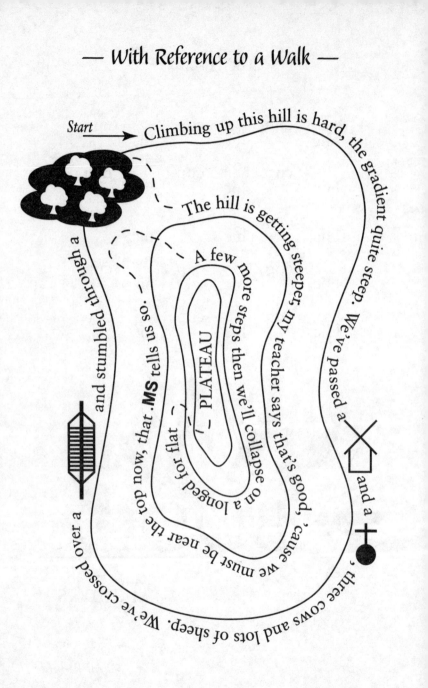

Start Climbing up this hill is hard, the gradient quite steep. We've passed a three cows and lots of sheep. We've crossed over a and stumbled through a The hill is getting steeper, my teacher says that's good, 'cause we must be near the top now, that .MS tells us so. A few more steps then we'll collapse on a longed for flat – PLATEAU and a

This poem relies on these symbols:

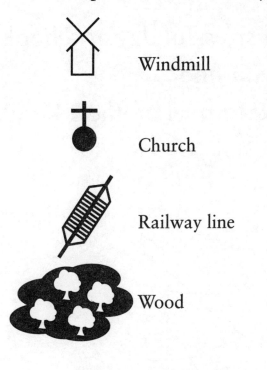

Windmill

Church

Railway line

Wood

.MS   Milestone

Footpath linking lines

Coral Rumble

After a stressful day at school
Don't you find
It's good to turn on the TV
And unwind

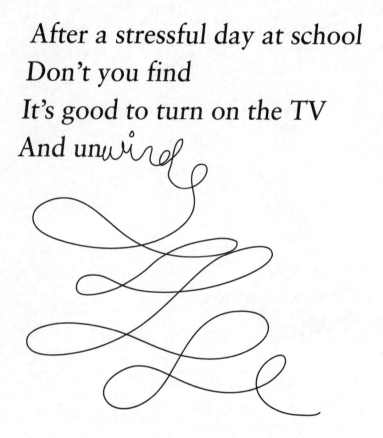

Roger Stevens

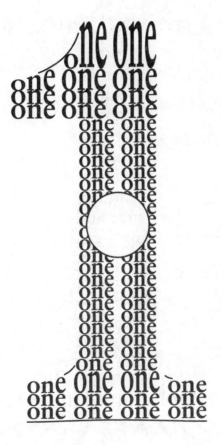

Fred Sedgwick

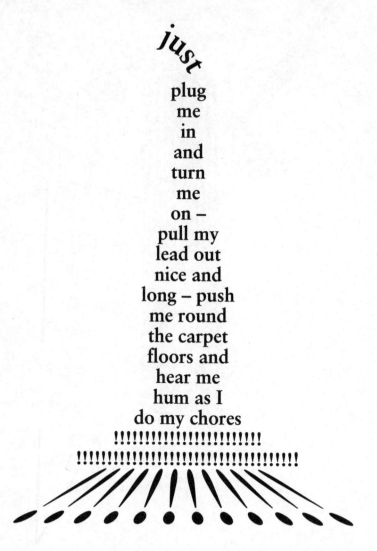

just
plug
me
in
and
turn
me
on –
pull my
lead out
nice and
long – push
me round
the carpet
floors and
hear me
hum as I
do my chores
!!!!!!!!!!!!!!!!!!!!!!!!
!!!!!!!!!!!!!!!!!!!!!!!!!!!!!!!!!!

James Carter

DENNIS

Dennis is the ice-
cream man – He drives
about in his ice-cream van

You always know when he's around
Because a) you can hear
that little tune he plays
from miles away –
and b) everyone
runs outside
screaming
'Hey, it's
Dennis
!!!'

James Carter

— Belt —

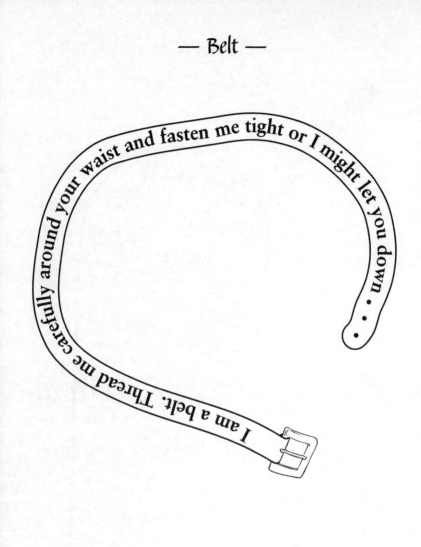

I am a belt. Thread me carefully around your waist and fasten me tight or I might let you down . . .

John Foster

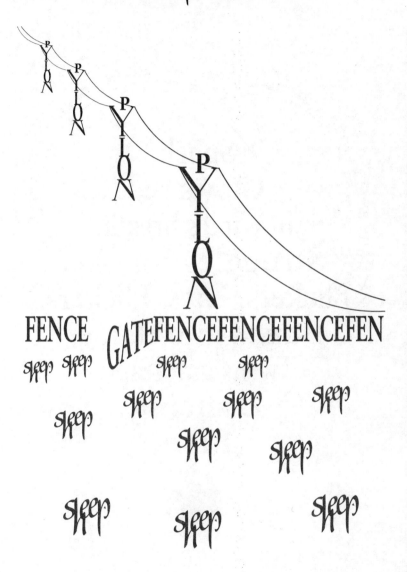

Alan Watkins-Groves

Spark
Glows red
In wind's breath.
Struggles for life.
Flickers. Dies. Flickers.
Bursts into flame.
Twists and leaps.
Dancing
Fire.

John Foster

— Size Poem —

microscopic
minuscule
teeny weeny
small
dinky
dainty
miniature
knee-high to a grasshopper

big
enormous
massive
huge
immense
gigantic
what a

WHOPPER!

Roger Stevens

— The River —

from a tiny spring the river came and wound it's way for days and days first west then east but always south always down even when it curled itself around a bend but then one day something changed as it ran so slow but free for the river grew and the river knew that now it was
THE SEA THE SEA THE SEA THE SEA THE SEA THE SEA THE
SEA THE SEA THE SEA THE SEA THE SEA THE SEA THE SEA
THE SEA THE SEA THE SEA THE SEA THE SEA THE SEA THE
SEA THE SEA THE SEA THE SEA THE SEA THE SEA THE SEA

James Carter

— Mexican Wave —

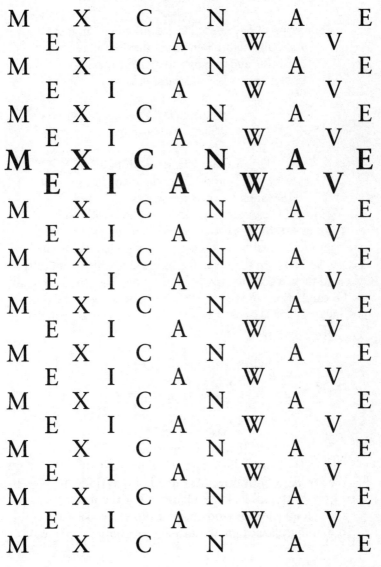

Philip Burton

— Sweet Dreams —

Sometimes I have peculiar dreams when I'm fast
Asleep at night. Sometimes they're full of
Ghosts and ghouls and give me quite
A fright. But the finest dreams I
Have when I am snug
Between my
Sheets are
The
Dreams that whisk me off to
Play in a land that's made of sweets.
In the land of sweets the streets are paved
With strawberry jam and the rivers flow with honey.
You can eat the chocolate trees for free no need to bring
Your money. All the lakes are made with lemonade and
The sea is filled with shandy. All the cars are fuelled with cans of
Coke and their wheels are made from candy. The clouds are balls
Of candy floss and the mud is chocolate mousse. All the
Chickens here lay Easter eggs and the rain is orange juice.
The mountain snow is whipped ice cream and the
Hills are apple crumble. If you stay around
Too long you'll find your tummy
Starts to rumble
Every house is built
From
Caramel and
The roofs are made
From cheesecake. Cold taps all
Flow with Pepsi Max and hot taps flow
With milkshake. And just as I'm about to
Eat a bed made from marshmallows I wake up
To find I've chewed my sheets and eaten both my pillows!

Ian Bland

Subtracting
Subtractin
Subtracti
Subtract
Subtrac
Subtra
Subtr
Subt
Sub
Su
S

<pre>
                              m   m   m
                           u   m u   u
                              l   l   l
Subt   t   t
Sub   i i   i
Su   p   p p   p
S   l   y   l
                        m   y i   i y y   y
                         u   i   n   i i   i
                         l   n   n   n
              mu l t i p l y i n g   g   g
                 l   p
                 u   l
                 t   y
                 i   i
                 p   n
                 l   g
                 y
mu l t i p l y i n g
                 g
</pre>

Ian Bland

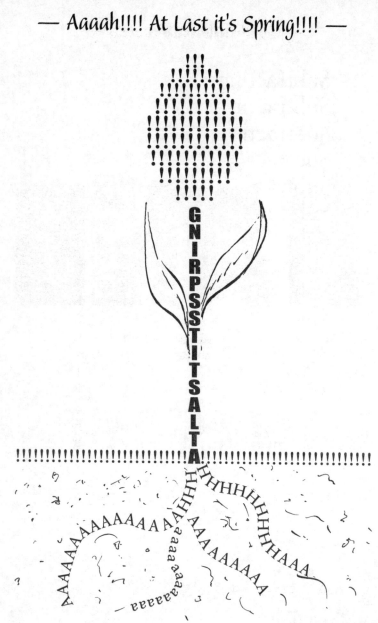

James Carter

=

BUS2H

Paul Cookson

I need no calendar:
one day in late Summer
one day much like another,
something in the light tilts;
the weather speaks deep
blood and feathers,
in my — tells me it's time to go.
I need no map, no lodestar:
the route home is printed
here in my curved wings;
my flight is urgent, slanted
free as the trade winds
singing Africa,
Africa

Tony Charles

40

— Africa —

THE SONG
THE BURNING SONG
THE DEMON VULTURES
THE HAZY TENTS   THE RAW
HORIZONS   THE DRUGGED SANDS   THE SCREAMING
THUNDER   THE RATTLING BONES   THE DUSTY MOUTHS
THE INFINITE EYES   THE DREAM POWER   THE CIRCLING
SKY   THE TREACHEROUS BIRDS   THE SHIFTING TOWNS THE
SNARLING GUNS   THE BURNING STORM   THE VAST RIVER   THE
CLAY DANCERS THE BLACK MASKS   THE RICH SANDS   THE HAZY
DEMON   THE SCREAMING SKIES   THE VULTURES MOUTHS   THE RAW
EYES   THE THUNDEROUS SONG   THE SHIFTING TRACKS   THE VAST
CIRCLE   THE RATTLING BIRDS   THE DUSTY TENTS   THE GUNS SNARL
THE STEAMING HORIZON   THE BONE FOREST   THE BURNING TOWNS   THE
SAND FLOWERS   THE TREACHEROUS INFINITE   THE BLACK TRACKED   THE
DANCERS SCREAM   THE MASKED GUNS   THE THUNDERS MOUTH   THE FOREST
TOWN   THE CLAY HUTS   THE STORMS POWER   THE DRUGGED RIVER   THE
SHIFTING SONGS THE SKYS EYE THE RATTLING DREAM THE SNARLING DUST THE
SANDS DEMONS THE BURNING BIRDS THE CIRCLING HAZE THE RAW BONES   THE
RICH TENTS   THE SCREAMING FLOWER   THE STEAMING CLAY   THE BLACK SAND
THE MASKED   DANCE THE TREACHEROUS HORIZON THE STORMS TRACK
THE RIVER THUNDER THE SHIFTY VULTURES THE
FORESTS POWER   THE RAW SKY THE SCREAMING
EYES   THE DREAM SONGS   THE DRUGGED HUTS
THE HAZY TOWNS   THE BURNT CIRCLE   THE
GUNS MOUTH   THE SNARLING BONES   THE
INFINITE BIRDS   THE DUSTY FLOWERS
THE STORMS MASK   THE THUNDERING
DEMONS   THE TENT DANCERS THE
RICH CLAY   THE SHIFTED POWER
THE SANDY RIVER   THE BURNING
TREACHERY THE RATTLING TRACK
THE BLACK STEAM THE POWERFUL
DREAM THE FLOWERING SONG THE
DRUGGED SCREAM THE DANCING EYE   THE
HORIZONTAL HUT THE MOUTHLESS   SNARLS
THE TRACKLESS SKY   THE RAW   FOREST
THE TENT TOWN THE HAZY   RIVER
THE INFINITE SHIFT   THE   BIRD
STORM   THE TREACHEROUS   DEMON
THE BURNING DRUG THE   GUN
DANCE   THE SINGING
BONE   THE MASKED
RICH   THE BLACK
CIRCLING THE
VAST   DREAM
SINGING

Dave Calder

— Shoe, Boot! Shoe! —

Dear Shoe, I've got
a crush on you,
I think you're
b-o-o-t-i-f-u-l.
Please, could you take a
shine to me or do you find me dull?
Dear Boot, you are a silly clog so kindly hold your tongue.
You are a heel and my soft soul, by you, will not be won.
Boot felt his throat tie in a knot. Shoe'd walked all over him
And now he's stashed back on the shelf,
alone,   out on a limb.

Gina Douthwaite

Concrete poems
are hard to read
Pneumatic
drills
are what
you need

Concrete poems are
hard to crack
It's builders who
have got the knack

John Foster

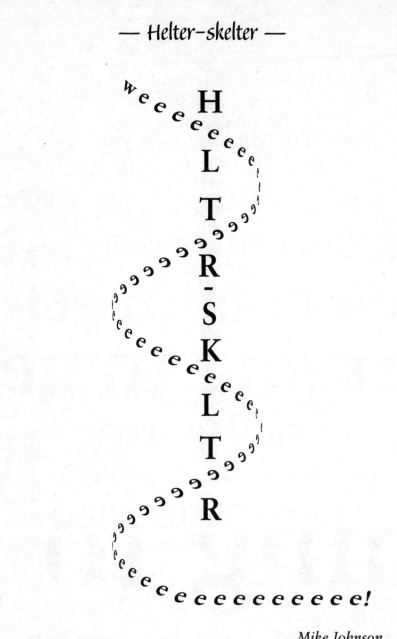

Mike Johnson

— Run —

I'm coming to get you
I'm coming to get you
I'm coming to get you
I'm coming to get you
I'm coming to get you
I'm coming to get you
I'm coming to get you
I'm coming to get you
I'm coming to get you

I'm coming to get you

m coming to get you

coming to get y

oming to get

ming to g

ning to g

Roger Stevens

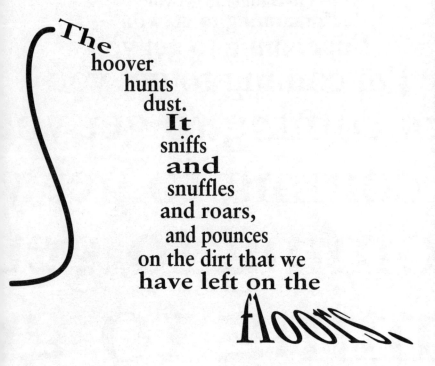

The
hoover
hunts
dust.
It
sniffs
and
snuffles
and roars,
and pounces
on the dirt that we
have left on the
floors.

Jill Townsend

— The Christmas Pudding —
from Start to Finish! —

Start at the bottom

pud!
Christmas
the
and light up
H
S
O
O
H
W
Pour
with a

Warm up
a ladle
of brandy,
with a
touch
match

Bubble it up
for an hour or two
turn it out.

Christmas day
hide it away till
hours – and – hours – then
On to the cooker to steam for
Swish, swish 'I wish . . .' don't tell!
TIME TO STIR AND MAKE A WISH!
in a bottle of rich dark stout and shout
Bang on the table, call everybody round, slosh
of dripping black treacle (go on, then, have a lick!).
of bright orange rind, one mug of brown sugar, and oodles
a few nuts, squeezes of lemon juice, small tangy curls
cooking apple (add a small carrot as well if you like). Next
red cherries and golden apricots. Grate up the suet and
Weigh out the glistening currants, sultanas, raisins,
nutmeg, angelica, sugary candied-peel.
flour and breadcrumbs, cinnamon
you might need: silky white
and gather everything
clear the table
First

Patricia Leighton

47

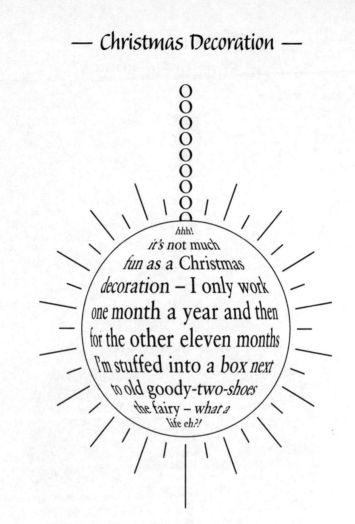

hhh!
it's not much
fun as a Christmas
decoration – I only work
one month a year and then
for the other eleven months
I'm stuffed into a *box next*
to old *goody-two-shoes*
the fairy – *what a*
life *eh?!*

James Carter

— Christmas Eve —

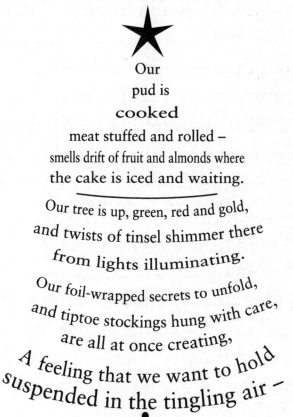

Our
pud is
cooked
meat stuffed and rolled –
smells drift of fruit and almonds where
the cake is iced and waiting.

Our tree is up, green, red and gold,
and twists of tinsel shimmer there
from lights illuminating.

Our foil-wrapped secrets to unfold,
and tiptoe stockings hung with care,
are all at once creating,

A feeling that we want to hold
suspended in the tingling air –

It's
Called
Anticipating.

Liz Brownlee

— Well-known Song Title —

The niiiiiiiiiiiiiiiiiiiiiiiiiiiiiiiiiiiiiiiiiiiiiiiiiiiiiii
iiiiiiiiiiiiiiiiiiiiiiiiiiiiiiiiiiiiiiiiiiiiiiiiiiiiiiiiiiiiii
iiiiiiiiiiiiiiiiiiiiiiiiiiiiiiiiiiiiiiiiiiiiiiiiiiiiiiiiiiiiii
iiiiiiiiiiiiiiiiiiiiiiiiiiiiiiiiiiiiiiiiiiiiiiiiiiiiiiiiiiiiii
iiiiiiiiiiiiiiiiiiiiiiiiiiiiiiiiiiiiiiiiiiiiiiiiiiiiiiiiiiiiii
iiiiiiiiiiiiiiiiiiiiiiiiiiiiiiiiiiiiiiiiiiiiiiiiiiiiiiiiiiiiii
iiiiiiiiiiiiiiiiiiiiiiiiiiiiiiiiiiiiiiiiiiiiiiiiiiiiiiiiiiiiii
iiiiiiiiiiiiiiiiiiiiiiiiiiiiiiiiiiiiiiiiiiiiiiiiiiiiiiiiiiiiii
iiiiiiiiiiiiiiiiiiiiiiiiiiiiiiiiiiiiiiiiiiiiiiiiiiiiiiiiiiiiii
iiiiiiiiiiiiiiiiiiiiiiiiiiiiiiiiiiiiiiiiiiiiiiiiiiiiiiiiiiiiii
iiiiiiiiiiiiiiiiiiiiiiiiiiiiiiiiiiiiiiiiiiiiiiiiiiiiiiiiiiiiii
iiiiiiiiiiiiiiiiiiiiiiiiiiiiiiiiiiiiiiiiiiiiiiiiiiiiiiiiiiiiii
iiiiiiiiiiiiiiiiiiiiiiiiiiiiiiiiiiiiiiiiiiiiiiiiiiiiiiiiiiiiii
iiiiiiiiiiiiiiiiiiiiiiiiiiiiiiiiiiiiiiiiiiiiiiiiiiiiiiiiiiiiii
iiiiiiiiiiiiiiiiiiiiiiiiiiiiiiiiiiiiiiiiiiiiiiiiiiiiiiiiiiiiii
iiiiiiiiiiiiiiiiiiiiiiiiiiiiiiiiiiiiiiiiiiiiiiiiiiiiiiiiiiiiii
iiiiiiiiiiiiiiiiiiiiiiiiiiiiiiiiiiiiiiiiiiiiiiiiiiiiiiiiiiiiii
iiiiiiiiiiiiiiiiiiiiiiiiiiiiiiiiiiiiiiiiiiiiiiiiiiiiiiiiiiight

(The Night Has A Thousand Eyes)
count them

Paul Cookson

— Family Tree —

This is our family tree

There's my Mum, my Dad and Me

Grandpa George and Grandma Jean

Uncle Joe and Aunt Irene

Cousin Tony and his son John

Auntie Betty and little Ron

There's distant relatives that I haven't met

There's due soon babies that aren't born yet

There's Aunties and Uncles, Dads and Mums

Nephews and Nieces and Brothers and Sons

It's easy to see where our family's going

With each new addition it keeps on growing

But if you want to see where our family's been

Just dig below the surface and the roots can be seen

Damian Harvey

51

— Crossword Puzzle —

CLUES:
2 down 3 across 5 down 6 across 7 across
1 across 6 down 3 down 4 down 4 across

7 across 1 across 6 down 3 down 4 down
5 down 4 across 2 down 3 across 6 across

4 down 5 down 4 across 7 across 1 across
6 down 3 down – 2 down 3 across 6 across

4 across 7 across 1 across 6 down 3 down
4 down – 2 down 3 across 5 down 6 across

2 down 3 across 6 across, 4 across 7 across
1 across 6 down 3 down 4 down – 5 down!

2 down 3 across 6 across 5 down 4 across
1 across 6 down 3 down 4 down 7 across

— Answers —

Paul Cookson

ANSWERS:

AS A SUPERB POET YOU CAN PLAY
AROUND WITH WORDS

YOU CAN PLAY AROUND WITH
SUPERB WORDS AS A POET

WITH SUPERB WORDS YOU CAN PLAY
AROUND – AS A POET

WORDS YOU CAN PLAY AROUND
WITH – AS A SUPERB POET

AS A POET, WORDS YOU CAN PLAY
AROUND WITH – SUPERB!

AS A POET SUPERB WORDS CAN PLAY
AROUND WITH YOU

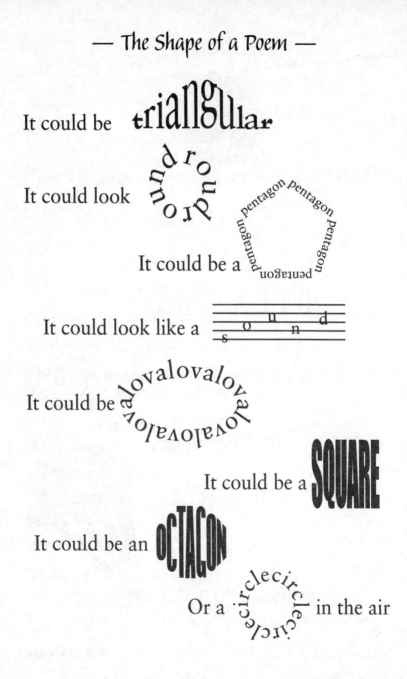

— The Shape of a Poem —

It could be **triaNGUlar**

It could look **round**

It could be a **pentagon**

It could look like a **sound**

It could be **ovalovalovaloval**

It could be a **SQUARE**

It could be an **OCTAGON**

Or a **circlecircle** in the air

It could be a **HEXAGON**

With six **straight sides**

Or a gently curving pattern

Like a **rollercoaster ride!**

But although these shapes are very **close**

Not one of them's quite ✔

For to me, the only shape

is when the poem's like a kite

Chris Ogden

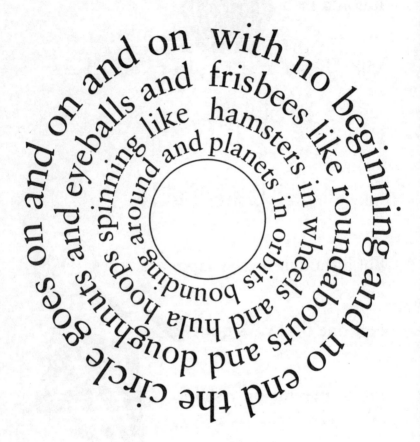

with no beginning and and no end the circle goes on and on and on and on and eyeballs and frisbees like roundabouts and doughnuts and hula hoops spinning like hamsters in wheels and planets in orbits bounding around

Suzanne Elvidge

— *o the wonderful shape of an o* —

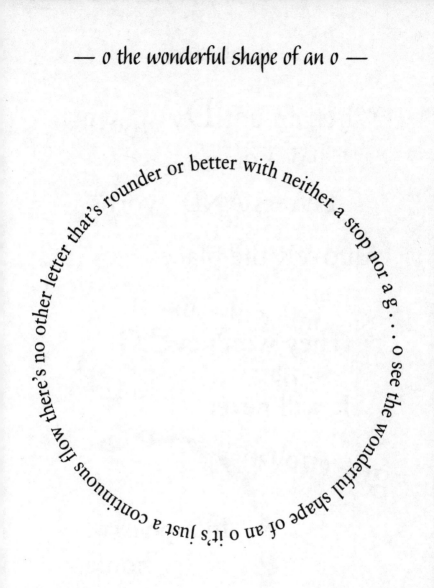

o see the wonderful shape of an o it's just a continuous flow there's no other letter that's rounder or better with neither a stop nor a g . . .

Rachel Rooney

— Untidy Poem —

Wh*a*t an untiDy   poem
It's a disgrace
Letters AND worbs

All oveR the place

No onE will   like it
They won't ev*en*
look
It will never

get PUblished

In a poetry
book

Roger Stevens

When standing up

is sitting there

though I leave the chair

a part of me still

David Petts

— Watch this Space! —

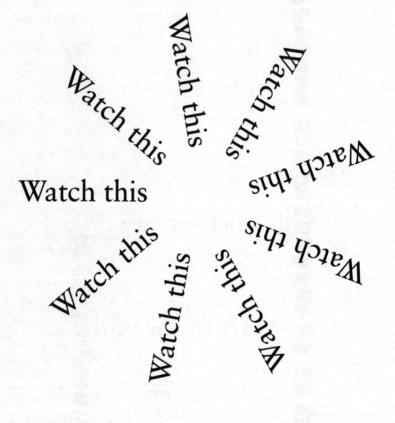

Judith Nicholls

— Tall Story —

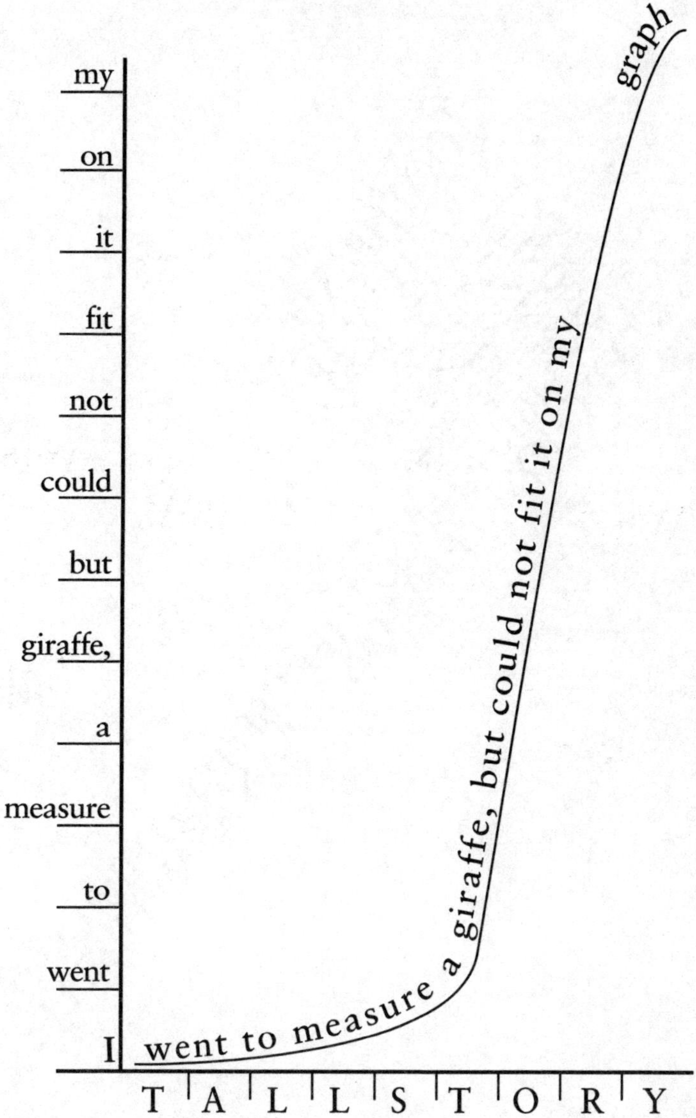
my
on
it
fit
not
could
but
giraffe,
a
measure
to
went
I
I went to measure a giraffe, but could not fit it on my graph
T A L L S T O R Y

Mike Johnson

— Teeth Cleaning Poem —

Sue Cowling

— Icicle —

long
tooth,
witch's
nail,
tip
of an
ice-
dragon's
tail,
sharp
horn,
drip
that
froze
at the
end of
an ice-
troll's
nose

o

Sue Cowling

Not wearing knickers, not navy, no more.

Want to wear silk ones 'cause cotton's a bore.

Want to wear pink ones with frills. I adore

not wearing knickers,   not navy, no more.

Gina Douthwaite

to claim part of it for their own!

Every

breaktime   boys

the

play

five-a-side

across

of

the   all

playground

never daring to stray away from the

walls and wondering if they'll ever be able

And all around the edge the girls stand,

Chris Ogden

— Toboggan —

Take me where the snow lies deep
On some hillside high and steep
Boldly sit astride my sleigh
One good push and I'm away.

Going speeding down the hill.

Getting faster – What a thrill!

At the bottom brush off snow.

Now to the top for another go.

David Whitehead

— *Owl* —

```
                            S
                       S  H
                    S  H  H
        O W L        S  H  H
      P R O W L S    L O W
      S H O W S    S L O W
        L O W   L O O P
          S W O O S H
          W H O O P S
          W O O O
        W O O O
      W O O
          W
  O O
  O O
```

Sandy Brownjohn

A storm is brewing and the air is crackling
Clouds are frowning dark and black
With a blinding flash and a deafening crash

LIGHTNING STRIKES STRAIGHT DOWN TO THE EARTH

Damian Harvey

— Begins with 'B' —

A bear?
A box?
A bin?
A bush?

A book?
A bomb?
A bus?
A brush?
A basket?
Boot?   A bit
of bread?   A
bone?   A bench?
A bouncy bed?
A badger's boil?
A blackbird's beak?
A bun? A bottom?
Building brick?

A bad banana?
Broken brolly? Biscuit
bitten by a bully?

Bubbles bursting in a
beaker? Bonny baby?
Bloomers? Beaver?

Bunch of bluebells?
Bee? A blot?
What is this shape?
What have I got?

Gina Douthwaite

— Building a Bonfire from the Bottom Up —

Start at the bottom

End.
Light.
Add the guy.
Build it higher.
Raid the tip for stuff.
Keep looking for stuff.
Penny for the guy, please missus.
Pray it doesn't rain the week before.
Dry leaves are good if you can find them.
You'll need to beg some spuds from your mams.
Nick from other bommies if you have to. Guard your own.

Next, cadge loads of newspapers and old wood from anyone you can.

Start: with a good piece of earthy ground well away from buildings and trees.

Angela Topping

— Whalespout —

The whale is a lyrical creature.
It knows all the songs from the shows
And please be aware
that it comes up for air
Spouting poetry!
See — Thar she blows!

Sue Cowling

— A Ride —

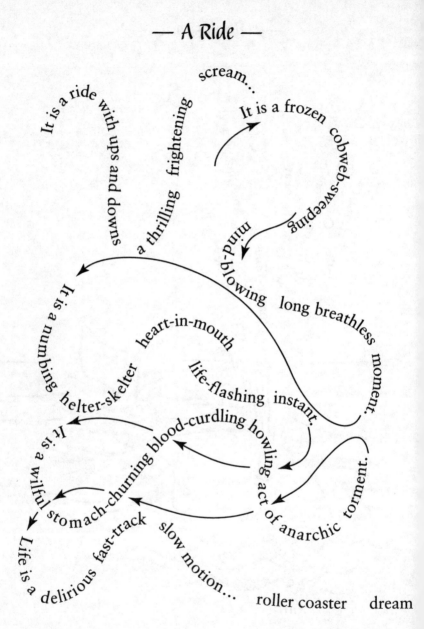

It is a ride with ups and downs
a thrilling frightening scream...
It is a frozen cobweb-sweeping
mind-blowing long breathless moment.
It is a numbing helter-skelter heart-in-mouth
life-flashing instant.
It is a wilful stomach-churning blood-curdling howling
act of anarchic torment.
Life is a delirious fast-track slow motion...
roller coaster dream

Debjani Chatterjee

— Bonfire —

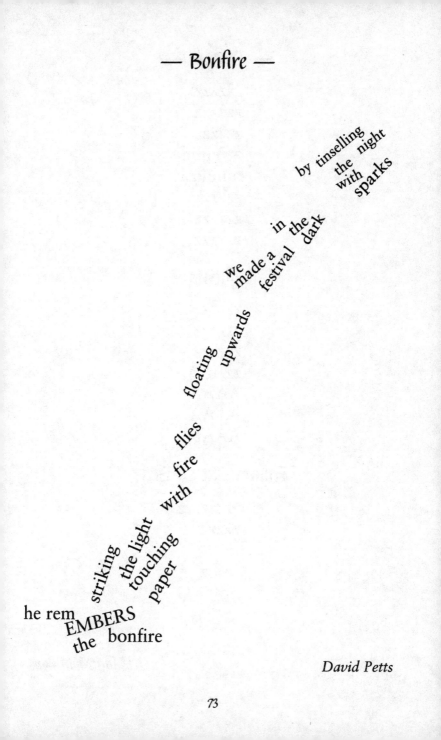

by tinselling
the night
with
sparks

we
made a in
festival the
dark

floating upwards

flies

fire

with

striking
the light
touching
paper

he rem
EMBERS
the bonfire

David Petts

— Dream —

zzzzzz
zzzzzz
zzzzzz
zzmmm
mmmzz
zzzzzz
zzzzzz
zzzzzz

Nightmare

zzzzzz
zzzzzz
zzzzzz
zzAAAA
AAAA
AAAA
AAAz

Falling Out Of Bed

zzzzzzzz
zzzzz
zz
   z
      O

Ian McMillan

Aaaa

When
you're
smitten by
a kitten, what's
your option?
One adoption!

Liz Brownlee

— Acknowledgements —

The publishers wish to thank the following for permission to use copyright material:

Ian Bland, 'Sweet Dreams', 'My Rocket Ship' and 'Calligrams' by permission of the author; **Paul Bright**, 'Step By Step' from *Here Come the Heebie Jeebies*, Hodder-Wayland (2000), bypermission of the author; **Sandy Brownjohn**, 'Owl' from *Both Sides of the Catflap*, Hodder Children's Books (1996), by permission of the author; **Liz Brownlee**, 'Buzz In', 'Purrfect', and 'Christmas Eve' by permission of the author; **Philip Burton**, 'Mexican Wave' by permission of the author; **Dave Calder**, 'Africa' and 'Pyramid' by permission of the author; **Richard Caley**, 'Somersault' by permission of the author; **Tony Charles**, 'Swallow' by permission of the author; **Debjani Chatterjee**, 'A Ride' by permission of the author; **Andrew Collett**, 'In the Bath' by permission of the author; **Sue Cowling**, 'Teeth Cleaning Poem' and 'Whalespout' by permission of the author and 'Icicle' from *A Mean Fish Smile*, Macmillan Children's Books Children's Books (2000), by permission of the author; **Gina Douthwaite**, 'Knickers', 'Shoe, Boot! Shoe' and CARtoon' from *Picture a Poem*, Random House Children's Books (1994) and 'Begins with B' from *Blueprint Poetry 3* (1997); **John Foster**, 'Belt', 'Child Skipping' and 'Ball Bouncing' from *Climb Aboard the Poetry Plane*, Oxford University Press (2000), copyright © John Foster 2000, 'Diamond Poem' from *The Works*, Macmillan Children's Books Children's Books (2000) copyright © John Foster 2000, 'Concrete Poems' from *Word Wizard*, Oxford University Press (2001), copyright John Foster 2001, all by permission of the author; **Damian Harvey**, 'Lightning Strikes' and 'Family Tree' by permission of the author; **Trevor Harvey**, 'Spaced Out' by permission of the author; **Mike Johnson**, 'Baked Beans: Special Offer' from *What Kind of Poem 2*, Collins (1999), by permission of the author, 'Tall Story' from *Dancing the Anaconda*, Beggis Books (1994), by permission of the author; **Pat Leighton**, 'Christmas Pudding' copyright Patricia Leighton © 2002 and 'Moon Journey' from *Christmas Poems*, Macmillan Children's Books (2000), both by permission of the author; **Ian McMillan**, 'Choir' from *The Invisible* Villain, Macmillan Children's Books (2002) and 'Dream', copyright © Ian McMillan, by permission of the author; **Tony Mitton**, 'Undersea Tea' copyright © 2002, by permission of the author; **Chris Ogden**, 'How Playtime Shapes Up' by permission of the author; **David Petts**, 'Bonfire' copyright © David Petts 2000 and 'Seated' copyright © David Petts 1999 by permission of the author; **Rachel Rooney**, 'o the wonderful shape of an o' by permission of the author; **Coral Rumble**, '*With Reference to a Walk' from Creatures, Teachers and Family Features*', Macdonald Young Books (1999), copyright Coral Rumble © 1997, 'The Hiccup' copyright Coral Rumble © 1994; **Fred Sedgwick**, 'A Golfing Success', from *Teaching Literacy: a creative approach*, Continuum, by permission of the author; **Roger Stevens**, 'Run', 'Size Poem' and 'Untidy Poem' by permission of the author, 'After School' from *I Did Not Eat the Goldfish*, Macmillan Children's Books (2002), by permission of the author; **Angela Topping**, 'Building a Bonfire' by permission of the author; **Jill Townsend**, 'The House Hunter' by permission of the author; **Alan Watkins-Groves**, 'The Open Gate' by permission of the author; **David Whitehead**, 'Toboggan' from *Secrets*, Ginn (1998), by permission of the author;

Every effort has been made to trace the copyright holders but if any have been inadvertently overlooked the publishers will be pleased to make the necessary arrangement at the first opportunity.

Dolphins Leap Lampposts

Dave Calder, Eric Finney and Ian Souter

All the very best from three performing poets sandwiched together in one tasty volume.

After Snow

Just a few footprints in the snow:
Yours perhaps? I wouldn't know.
I'm certain that they are not mine.
First-footing in new snow is fine,
But waking to that dazzling white
After secret snow at night,
I'd wonder at a world new-minted
And leave perfection quite unprinted.

Eric Finney

Poems for Year 3

CHOSEN BY PIE CORBETT

Poems for Year 3 features poems which relate to all elements of the Literacy Strategy for Year 3, including poems of observation, poems about the senses, poems for performance and poems which are packed with humour. It is a beautiful collection featuring stunning pieces from poets as varied as John Agard, John Foster, Roger McGough, Langston Hughes, Emily Dickinson, Ted Hughes and Charles Causley.

Alien Lullaby

Hush, little alien, don't you cry!
Mamma's gonna bake you a moonbeam pie

And if that moonbeam pie goes stale
Mamma's gonna catch you a comet's tail

And if that comet's tail won't flip
Mamma's gonna make you a rocket ship

And if that rocket ship won't stay
Mamma's gonna buy you the Milky Way

And if the Milky Way's too far
Mamma's gonna bring you a shooting star

And if that shooting star falls down –
You're still the sweetest little alien in town!

Sue Cowling

Poems for Year 4

CHOSEN BY PIE CORBETT

Poems for Year 4 features poems which relate to all elements of the Literacy Strategy for Year 4 including poems on specific themes, poems using figurative language, modern poems, classic poems and poems from other cultures. It is a beautiful collection featuring stunning pieces from poets as varied as George Szirtes, Langston Hughes, Kit Wright, Helen Dunmore, John Agard, Roger McGough, Christina Rossetti and Charles Causley.

Miss! Sue is Kissing

Miss! Sue is kissing
the tadpoles again.
She is, Miss. I did,
I asked her. She said
something about catching
him young. Getting one
her own age. I don't know,
Miss. She keeps whispering
'Prince, Prince.' Isn't that
a dog's name, Miss?

Michael Harrison

The Works

Every kind of poem you will ever need for the Literacy Hour

chosen by Paul Cookson

The Works really does contain every kind of poem you will ever need for the Literacy Hour but it is also a book packed with brilliant poems that will delight any reader.

It's got chants, action verses, riddles, tongue-twisters, shape poems, puns, acrostics, haikus, cinquains, kennings, couplets, thin poems, lists, conversations, monologues, epitaphs, songs, limericks, tankas, nonsense poems, raps, narrative verse and performance poetry, and that's just for starters.

It features poems from the very best classic and modern poets, for example:
William Blake, Michael Rosen, Robert Louis Stevenson, Allan Ahlberg, W.H. Auden, Brian Patten, Roger McGough, Roald Dahl, Charles Causley, Eleanor Farjeon, Benjamin Zephaniah, Ted Hughes, T.S. Eliot and William Shakespeare to name but a few.

A book packed with gems for dipping in to time and time again.

The Works 2

Pie Corbett and Brian Moses

The Works 2 really does contain poems for every primary school subject and occasion but it is also a book packed with fantastic poems that will delight any reader. It is a wonderfully well-crafted anthology which relates literacy work across the curriculum.

It has poems about Maths, Science, Geography, History, Religious Education, Information Technology, Design and Technology, Music and Art – plus good choices for assemblies and other themes such as citizenship and the environment. It also has a section dealing with subjects such as bullying, a new baby, death, changing school and making friends.

It features poems from the very best classic and modern poets, for example:
Langston Hughes, William Shakespeare, Eleanor Farjeon, Charles Causley, Brian Patten, Roger McGough, Christina Rosetti, Benjamin Zephaniah, Jackie Kay, T.S. Eliot, Ted Hughes and Michael Rosen to name but a few.

A book packed with gems for dipping into time and time again.

ARE YOU SITTING COMFORTABLY?

chosen by Brian Moses

Are You Sitting Comfortably? is a wonderful collection of story poems covering an incredible range of topics from Alexander III of Scotland to Sleeping Beauty via the delight that is A Visit to Yalding.

from

The Tomcat of Notre Dame

High above the roofs of Paris
Lives the Tomcat of Notre Dame
Looking down at the passers-by
Ready to save them from harm

The river Seine below him
He watches the boats go by
All set to swing to the rescue
In a twinkling of an eye

Catching a baby pigeon
Or a puppy from under a bus
Saving a drowning kitten
Never making a fuss

Adrian Henri